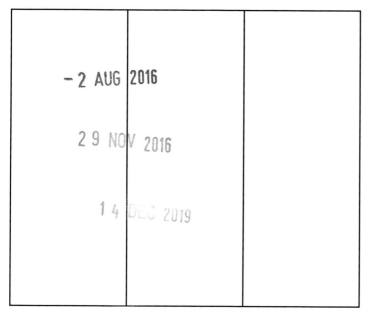

AMBERLEY

First published 2016

Amberley Publishing
The Hill, Stroud
Gloucestershire, GL5 4EP

www.amberley-books.com

ISBN 978 1 4456 5903 9 (print)
ISBN 978 1 4456 5904 6 (ebook)

British Library Cataloguing in Publication Data.
A catalogue record for this book is available from
the British Library.

Typeset in 9.5pt on 12pt Celeste.
Typesetting by Amberley Publishing.
Printed in the UK.

Acknowledgements

My first book, *The Buses of Northern Scottish*, covered the buses operated by Northern Scottish in the north-east of Scotland, generally within the Grampian area. This book essentially covers the same area but features the buses and coaches of the independent operators from the seventies and onwards. One or two earlier images are included where appropriate.

Most of the images printed here were taken by me, but some have been acquired elsewhere. I am indebted to James Mair and Ewan Wood for allowing me to use some of their images. Any copyright infringement is unintentional.

To all the operators I have spoken to or visited over the years – thank you so much for allowing me access to your premises to photograph your vehicles. Thank you for updating me on fleet changes. Thank you for the odd 'shotty', whether it was something new or something interesting, and thank you for sharing your photographs with me – one or two are included in this book.

PSV Circle fleet books, TAG fleet books, and bus lists on the Web have been used to verify some details.

Finally, thanks to my wife Jean for her patience, sitting in the car outside operator yards while I took photographs and claiked with operators and drivers, and also for helping me proof-check before going to print.

Background

I started taking an interest in the local independent bus and coach operators around the late seventies, at a time when I was a driver with Alexanders Northern. A lot of my photographs were therefore taken 'covertly', as I was concerned that operators might question why an Alexanders employee would want to photograph their vehicles. Towards the end of the eighties, a career change took me to work with Grampian Regional Council in a post that would see me have near daily contact with most, if not all, of the local independents. It was at that time that I realised these established, small, and sometimes not so small, operators were run by extremely hardworking families, and were not the here-today-gone-tomorrow outfits that the large bus groups would have had everyone believe.

In the past, most towns and villages had a local bus/coach operator, whose business was more than likely linked to the local car repair garage, petrol station, village shop or hotel. Many of the rural operators started off providing taxi and car hire services after the Second World War, expanding in to minibuses and big buses as demand for local outings increased. The backbone of the bus and coach business was usually the daily transportation of school pupils, with some local service work if a road service licence was granted. Evening and weekend hires would keep the wheels turning. Operators based in the fishing ports also gained valuable seasonal work in transferring boat crews from their home port to various ports on the west coast, and at times to ports on the south coast of England. Before the mass availability of the family car, the annual bus trip to the picnic was the only opportunity for many children to pass beyond their town or village boundary.

Public bus services in the north-east were operated on the same basis as elsewhere in Scotland, the majority operated by companies within the nationalised Scottish Bus Group, W. Alexander & Sons (Alexanders Northern post-1961, Northern Scottish post-1985) being the main operator for the north-east. Although the deregulation of bus services in the mid-eighties saw some competition on more profitable routes, there was no competition on the rural routes. The advent of subsidised services did, however, give smaller operators the opportunity to run some of the rural services that the Scottish Bus Group companies deemed uneconomic to operate, with the security of a contract payment, no matter how busy or quiet the route was. Notable competition in this area came from Grampian Transport, the privately owned former Aberdeen-based municipal operator who started services on the Ellon, Inverurie, Westhill, Newmachar and Stonehaven routes in 1986. By late 1987, competition between the two companies came to an end. Alexanders North East was a new company created by former Alexander Northern managers in 1988. To get services started, they acquired the Dyce-based Glenhire Coaches business. They used a mix of their coaches and coaches hired in from other operators, pending the introduction of new high-quality coaches, on routes to Fraserburgh and Peterhead initially, expanding their operations to Stonehaven soon after. Competition from this new organisation was short lived, however, when the company collapsed mid-November 1989. A later entrant to the Buchan routes was Peterhead-based Rogers Coaches, who branded their services ACE – Aberdeen Commuter Express – but after fierce retaliation from the incumbent operator, Stagecoach Bluebird, the competing services were cancelled.

Today there are a very small number of what could be classed as competing services – small beer in comparison with previous competitive skirmishes. Bain's Coaches operate between Oldmeldrum and Aberdeen, while Deveron Coaches operate the Banff/Macduff town service.

In the sixties and seventies the fleet profile for most of the independent operators would have been second-hand acquisitions, mainly Bedfords and Fords. Seddon and AEC vehicles could be found, Leyland was quite a rare breed. New coaches were mainly sourced through the bus grant scheme, where vehicles had to be fitted with power doors and used for a period on public services. Double-deckers were rare at this time, with only Reid's of Rhynie and Frasers of Elgin opting to use such vehicles. That would change – towards the end of the eighties and during the nineties and beyond many operators would acquire second-hand deckers, mainly Volvo Ailsas, for school contract work. Circumstances would change, however, as customers expected high-quality coaches and, with greater VOSA legislation and attention, operators started acquiring more robust Volvo, Scania and Dennis products.

In preparing this book, I did a quick count on PSV operators whom I have known existed from the seventies until today – I counted over ninety and I am sure I will have forgotten some. Today there are far less. In an effort to consolidate their dominant status, both Grampian Transport and Bluebird Buses embarked on takeovers. Aberdeen-based Mair's Coaches and Banchory-based Kirkpatrick Coaches went under the Grampian umbrella, as did some of the remnants of the failed Alexanders North East and Glenhire Coaches. Stagecoach-owned Bluebird Buses were considerably more active during the mid-nineties, acquiring Norrie's Coaches of New Deer, Hardie's Coaches of Aberchirder, Easton's Coaches of Inverurie, MacLean's Coaches of Portknockie, Gray's Coaches of Fochabers, and Scotravel of Elgin. Others like Cruickshank's Coaches of Ellon, Victoria Coaches of Macduff, Smith's Coaches of Keith and Roberts of Rothiemay have simply shut the door and sold their vehicles. The longest serving companies in the area would include Maynes Coaches of Buckie, established 1947, and J. C. Keir of Glass, established around the same time as a taxi operator, buying their first coach soon after.

The takeovers and closures may well have benefited others – notably, operators such as Maynes Coaches of Buckie, Kineil Coaches and Watermill Coaches of Fraserburgh, Deveron Coaches of Macduff and Central Coaches of Aberdeen have greatly expanded over the years, all starting from a small scale and enjoying significant growth over the last twenty years or so. Despite the takeovers and closures, no new entrants other than taxi and minibus operators have taken the plunge in the local bus and coach market.

This book is not a comprehensive history of north-east independents – unfortunately, my photograph and slide collection does not cover every operator in the area. It covers those for which I have images, with illustrations selected to reflect the variety of vehicles types and vehicle types that were less common in this area. Hopefully it will serve as a reminder of companies and vehicles that no longer serve our communities.

A & I Coaches, Stonehaven. Established as a taxi company, A & I expanded into coaches towards the late nineties. L251 BGA was a thirty-five-seat Setra. It departed the fleet during 2014.

A & I Coaches, Stonehaven. Toyota Caetano H386 DAS was acquired from Highland Scottish in 1995. I last saw this vehicle around three years ago, on a croft near Bridge of Marnoch.

Aberdeen Coach Hire, Aberdeen. This company was set up by Alan Laing in 1987, but the venture only lasted around two years. NDV 44W was a 1980 Bedford YMT, new to Tillingbourne Coaches, and is seen in Aberdeen with Alan Laing behind the wheel.

AJS Enterprizes, Cruden Bay. Established by Jim Smith, the company also traded as Cruden Bay Coaches, operating subsidised services and contract hires in and around Aberdeen. Ex-United Counties ECW-bodied Leyland Leopard CNH173X was acquired for a night-bus contract from Aberdeen, but had been allocated to daytime service work when photographed.

AJS Enterprizes, Cruden Bay. Former Ribble Duple Dominant bodied Leyland Leopard WCK 135V was operating the Aberdeen Airport/city centre service when photographed at Aberdeen Airport.

Alexander North East, Aberdeen. Following the collapse of the business in 1990, the fleet was transferred from their Dyce depot into the council compound at Portlethen, pending the resolution of a dispute between the council and the company. Scania B686 NSG was eventually sold to Allan & Black, Aboyne.

Alexander North East, Aberdeen. F106 SSE was the first of a batch of five Ikarus-bodied Volvo B10M coaches acquired in the spring of 1989 for the Stonehaven corridor services. It is seen on delivery on the A1.

Alexander North East, Aberdeen. As well as the coaches for their service network, the company also acquired two former Scottish Bus Group Alexander-bodied Leyland Leopard buses for school contract work. This one-time Alexander Midland, Kelvin Scottish, Stagecoach Magicbus vehicle also went to auction following the collapse of the company.

Allan & Black, Aboyne. The Bedford VAL with twin steer was a fairly uncommon choice for operators in this area. One of the few to operate such a coach was Allan & Black, who ran this 1965 Duple-bodied example.

Allan & Black, Aboyne. Another unusual type for a north-east operator was this 1986 Metroliner, new as C217 KMA to Crosville.

Allan & Black, Aboyne. One of the most recent purchases is BVS 118, a forty-eight-seat Neoplan Starliner coach, new as YR02 UOF to Hallmark Coaches.

Allan & Black, Aboyne. Yet another rarity for this area, Alexander-bodied Scania G369 RTO, new to Nottingham City Transport. It is seen here in Torphins, operating a school contract, in June 2005.

Amber Travel, Turriff. Established in 1989, the company originally operated from the old Alexander's garage at Markethill, Turriff. They subsequently moved to Crossfields on the outskirts of Turriff, where former Stables of Keith Dennis Javelin NUI 2420 (originally N883 JRE) is seen.

Amber Travel, Turriff. One of the last vehicles acquired before the company closed was Bova R748 TWR.

ARMA Travel, Aberdeen. TYG 442R was a Duple-bodied Bedford YLQ, new to Steel, Addingham in 1977, and acquired by Arma Travel to operate a competing service with Northern Scottish during the early eighties. The venture did not last long, however.

Bain's Coaches, Oldmeldrum. Established 1975, the company was originally based at Kemnay but moved to Oldmeldrum during the nineties. This 1986 image sees Duple-bodied Ford WED 981S arriving at Prospecthill Road in Glasgow with Aberdeen FC supporters attending a cup final at nearby Hampden Park on 10 May 1986.

Bain's Coaches, Oldmeldrum. Attending the same Aberdeen *v.* Hearts cup final (3-0 win for Aberdeen) is Bain's Plaxton-bodied Leyland Leopard 538 UYC, new in 1974 to Limebourne of London as GNM 223N.

Bain's Coaches, Oldmeldrum. Bain's operate a small network of commercial and subsidised bus services, in addition to school contract and private hire work. One of the vehicles acquired for service work was Optare Delta S306 KNW, a one-time member of the Birmingham-based Claribels fleet. It is currently out of service.

Bain's Coaches, Oldmeldrum. JIL 7656 is a Marcopolo-bodied MAN coach, acquired in 2013 from VIP Travel, Aughton where it carried the registration PN05 DZH.

Balgownie Coaches, Aberdeen. Seen at Fochabers during the mid-seventies, this 1966 AEC Reliance was new to Pritchard, London.

Balgownie Coaches, Aberdeen. Seen at the same location as the previous image, this AEC Reliance was new to Nottingham-based Barton Transport in 1966.

Berry's of Fyvie, Fyvie. NSB300J was a 1971 Bedford YRQ with Duple Viceroy body, new to West Coast Motors of Campbeltown. This mid-seventies image shows it at their rural depot on the outskirts of Fyvie.

Berry's of Fyvie, Fyvie. A later acquisition was OPP 904P, a 1976 Duple-bodied Bedford YMT new to Tricentrol Coaches of Dunstable. It would see further service with the Welsh Dragon Coaches of Port Talbot.

Betaway Travel, Balmedie. Based in Balmedie they opted for second-hand heavy-weight coaches, including an AEC and two Seddon coaches for school contract and private hire work. Plaxton-bodied Seddon NEK 31K was a rare beast, new to Smith of Wigan in 1972. The coach then went to Berry of Fyvie for further service. It then languished at Berry's yard for many a year before, I believe, it went for scrap around 2011.

Betaway Travel, Balmedie. Carrying a later-style front grille is YSU 910, a Plaxton-bodied AEC Reliance, new as WDK 648K to Yelloway Coaches.

Brown's of Macduff, Macduff. Established in the early seventies, they had one of the most varied fleets in the area at that time, including second-hand AEC and Bristol saloons, as well as new Volvo, Leyland, Bedford and Setra coaches. This Park Royal bodied AEC Reliance started life with East Kent in 1964.

Brown's of Macduff, Macduff. Their last new purchase was CRS 327Y, a forty-nine-seat executive class Setra purchased in 1983. It is seen on West Cathcart Street in Buckie.

Burns Coaches, Tarves. Despite displaying Travel Dundee logos, this Volvo Ailsa was being used on school contract work by Burns when photographed at the bus parking area at Inverurie Academy during 2003.

Burns Coaches, Tarves. As well the usual mix of contract and local hire work, Burns have operated a comprehensive tour programme using high-quality coaches. Acquired in 2007 for tours, their one and only Setra coach SV07 AZZ is seen heading out of Portsoy on a private hire during the summer of 2013.

Burr's Coaches, Whitehills. Seen in withdrawn condition in 1978 at Whitehills, this 1960 Bedford SB1 had been inherited by Burr's when they took over the Ritchie's Coaches business. This particular coach was new to Makinson of Moston.

Burr's Coaches, Whitehills. UTY 692H sits opposite the Harbour Garage. This was a 1970 Plaxton-bodied Bedford SB5, new to St Mary's Hospital in Morpeth.

C & M Coaches, Fyvie. C & M operated contract work in Fyvie and Turriff area. Their final two vehicles are seen at Backhill, Fyvie, after the company closed. This 1984 Ford was acquired by C & M from Bluebird Buses when they took over Norrie's of New Deer. It still survives today, used as a static office at a Brechin equestrian centre.

Cadger's Coaches (Drew Cadger), Peterhead. VRY 357 was a 1984 Van Hool-bodied Volvo B10M, new to Cotters Tours of Glasgow. It was subsequently operated by Fraserburgh-based Watermill Coaches after they took over the Cadger business in 1992.

Cadgers Coaches (Robert Cadger), Belhelvie. GSS 703V was a 1980 Bedford YLQ with Plaxton body. It is seen on a football hire to Glasgow, May 1986.

Cadgers Coaches (Robert Cadger), Belhelvie. This 1990 PMT-bodied Mercedes 811D was also bought new by the company. It is seen heading down Union Street in Aberdeen.

Central Coaches, Aberdeen. This company started in 1984 as a taxi company, expanding into minibuses and coaches from 2004. For tendered service work, the company acquired this former Eirebus Optare Solo, originally registered 07-D-39306.

Central Coaches, Aberdeen. An increase in school contracts has seen a significant expansion of the coach fleet. Two of these are seen parked at Bridge of Don in February 2016. Nearest the camera is L70 CTC, a Van Hool-bodied Volvo, while furthest from the camera is R301 BJA, a Plaxton-bodied Volvo.

Central Coaches, Aberdeen. D5 CTC was new to Marbill of Beith as T9 MCS. It is a Van Hool-bodied Volvo B10M-55 tri-axle coach.

Cheyne's Coaches, Daviot (Inverurie). Acquired from Saltcoats-based Clyde Coast in 1985, 3492 TU was a 1980 Volvo B58 with Plaxton Viewmaster body new to Monks of Leigh as BBN869V. Withdrawn by Cheyne's in 1993, it saw further service with Reid's of Rhynie.

Cheyne's Coaches, Daviot (Inverurie). JOV 703P was a MCW-bodied Bristol VRT, acquired from Marshall, Ballieston, in 1991, but new to West Midlands PTE in 1975.

Cheyne's Coaches, Daviot (Inverurie). This 2016 view shows three of the fleet at the Daviot depot with Bova C3 CHT nearest the camera, and two Van Hool-bodied Volvo coaches keeping it company. C3 CHT was originally T343 NBV, OTC 950 originally R609 CJS, and VRG 939 originally M873 GYS.

Clarks Coaches, Banchory. Clark's operated a mixed fleet of second-hand buses and coaches that included Leyland, AEC and Bedford examples. Seen in Glasgow April 1983, it would have been a long and probably noisy journey in this wee Bedford VAS5. It was new in 1972 to Horlock of Northfleet.

Clarks Coaches, Banchory. Three years later and football supporters would have had the luxury of this Plaxton-bodied AEC Reliance for the trip to Hampden. 9875 MZ was new in 1971 to Wallace Arnold as AUA 434J.

Clarks Coaches, Banchory. The owner at work. Fred Clark attends to the brakes of recently acquired Bedford YLQ ASR 657T in this 1988 view. The coach had previously worked for Midland, Auchterarder but was new as YSP 477T to Watson of Dundee in 1979.

Cruickshank's of Ellon, Ellon. In use as a store at the Ellon depot in 1977, this Burlingham-bodied Bedford SB is believed to be former Alexander's EMS 830.

Cruickshank's of Ellon, Ellon. Seen at Banchory on a summer outing with local pensioners is A129 SNH, a 1984 Jonckheere-bodied DAF new to Rowley, Emerson Park, but acquired from Rosendale, Northolt, in 1986.

Dawson's Bus Service, Stuartfield. Tom Dawson ran this Duple-bodied Volvo B10M, originally NCS 125W when it served as a London night coach with Western SMT.

Deveron Coaches, Macduff. Like a lot of other companies, Deveron started out as a taxi operator trading as Margaret's Taxis. They expanded into larger capacity vehicles around 1993, and in recent years have opened new depots in Buckie and Keith in response to additional school contract work. This former Tayside Volvo Ailsa was acquired in 1998 for a contract to Buckie High School. The all-grey livery has since been replaced. It is seen parked up between school runs at Ianstown, Buckie.

Deveron Coaches, Macduff. A number of subsidised services have been operated over the years. In this view we see East Lancs-bodied Volvo B6 on the A98 near Fochabers as it sets out on one of the services in the snow of December 2009.

Deveron Coaches, Macduff. A number of these former Wallace Arnold Jonckheere-bodied Volvo B12M coaches were acquired in 2012. GT03 MMM is seen at the Buckie depot.

Deveron Coaches, Macduff. Acquired in 2015, this King Long coach is currently the newest coach in the fleet. It is seen at Macduff.

Pat Duff, Cullen. This 1971 Plaxton-bodied Bedford SB was acquired for a school contract between Cullen and Buckie High School. This was an unusual purchase as, by 1971, this style of Plaxton body combined with the SB chassis looked quite dated. The vehicle went on to work for Fraser's of Elgin, eventually being sold to Robertson's of Elgin for the transportation of their workers to various house-building sites in the area.

Dunbar's Coaches, Elgin. Jim 'Nipper' Dunbar started operating taxis from his Palace Garage premises in Elgin in 1963. Over the years he moved into minibuses, and then full-size coaches. OWP 25P was an extremely rare coach. New in 1976, it had a rear engine based on Bedford YRQ running units, with a Caetano Cascais body. Only eight of these were imported from the Portuguese coachbuilder.

Easton's Coaches, Inverurie. New in 1971, this Willowbrook-bodied Ford R192 would have been acquired using the bus grant scheme, which required vehicles to have a power-operated door and be used for a certain time on service work.

Easton's Coaches, Inverurie. Seen having just been delivered to the coach painter at Aultmore, near Keith, is Caetano-bodied DAF WGA 624W.

Forres Minicoaches, Forres. This one-time Maynes of Buckie Plaxton-bodied Scania is seen at their depot in Forres. It was originally registered K777 KGM.

Forres Minicoaches, Forres. A number of vehicles were parked up after the company closed in 2013. The two shown here are Marshall-bodied Dennis Dart N602 XRJ, new to Manchester Airport, and Irizar-bodied Scania P983 LKL, new to Kings Ferry.

Fraser's Coaches, Elgin. Joe Fraser started running buses in 1964 and bought his first full-size coach, a Duple Firefly bodied Ford, in 1965. He took over the business of Hay's Bus Service in 1968, and adopted the Fraser's Coaches name from that time. In 1972 he bought this Duple Viceroy bodied Ford R192, seen at his original premises behind Elgin town hall.

Fraser's Coaches, Elgin. In 1974 he moved to purpose-built premises on Grampian Road in Elgin, where three of his coaches are seen in this 1978 image. The business closed in 1981 and the premises were sold to a joinery business. Within the last two years or so, the entire area has been acquired for flood alleviation. The garage has subsequently been demolished.

Fraser's Coaches, Elgin. Fraser's Plaxton-bodied Bedford VAS5 is seen at the Forres depot next to the old Plasmon meal mill. The coach was new in 1975.

Fraser's Coaches, Elgin. Over the years Joe Fraser operated two double-deckers, ex-Potteries Daimler XVT 675 and this splendid ex-City of Oxford AEC Renown 342 TJO.

G & M Coaches, Whitehills. Following on from Ritchie's and Burr's of Whitehills, George Lawrence operated his coach business from the Harbour Garage. TBC 227 was one of two Bova coaches operated, this being the EL26 variant, originally registered CSO 130Y. The second Bova, E908 NSE, was the FLD variant and featured the more bulbous front end.

Glenhire/Fountain Executive, Aberdeen. Glenhire have always operated high-class executive-type coaches, exploiting the lucrative private hire and contract market associated with Aberdeen-based oil companies. Neoplans were their favoured choice for many a year and an early example was this short N907 model, new in 1982.

Glenhire/Fountain Executive, Aberdeen. In 1988 Glenhire sold out to Alexanders North East, a new company set up to compete with Northern Scottish, the main provider of local bus services in the north-east. Following the collapse of the company, the former owner of Glenhire re-entered the business trading as Fountain Executive, again using high-quality coaches for corporate hires. MIB 1092 typifies the type of coaches operated by Fountain, this being a 1983 Neoplan new to Bergland of Watford.

Glenhire/Fountain Executive, Aberdeen. Scania FXI 214 passes Tormore Distillery on the A95 during the summer of 2015.

Glennie of Keith, Keith. Eric Glennie started his motor-hire business in the late forties, acquiring his first bus in 1954. As well as the normal hire and school work, some services were operated, thereby allowing vehicles to be purchased using the bus grant scheme available in the seventies. One such vehicle was Plaxton-bodied Bedford YRQ NSE4L, new in 1972. The coach is seen parked at Lossie Green car park in Elgin and clearly shows the 'bus grant' type door that had to be fitted to qualify for the grant.

Glennie of Keith, Keith. Another Bedford purchased new was CSE 122T, a 1978 Bedford YLQ. It is seen in Glasgow on 21 May 1983 with football supporters attending the Scottish Cup final – Aberdeen beat Rangers 1-0.

G. B. Gray, Fochabers. SDS 663R was a tidy Duple-bodied Ford R1014, new in 1976 to Doherty of Cambuslang.

Hans Hardie, Hardie's Coaches, Aberchirder. Hans Hardie was one of the few operators in the area to run the Bedford Val. YNK 636F was one of a pair of Duple-bodied examples, and from memory these had been converted to Leyland power at some point in their life. It was new in 1968 to Biss of Bishops Stortford.

Hans Hardie, Hardie's Coaches, Aberchirder. Hardie's also took advantage of the bus grant, acquiring this Plaxton-bodied Bedford YRQ in 1974. It is seen in Buckie on a private hire.

Hans Hardie, Hardie's Coaches, Aberchirder. Hardie's sold out to Bluebird Buses in 1994. One of the coaches that transferred to the new owner was XRM 772Y, seen here at the Aberchirder base just before the takeover. This Duple-bodied Leyland Leopard was new in 1983 to Abbott of Workington.

Hay's Coaches, Drumblade, Huntly. Another rare type to operate in the area was CSU 977, a Plaxton-bodied Bristol LH new to Western National as SFJ 132R.

Hay's Coaches, Drumblade, Huntly. Seen being washed at the Drumblade depot is KGG 661V, a Ford T152 with Plaxton body, new in 1979 to Crawford of Neilston.

Irene's Coaches/Newmachar Coaches, Newmachar. FWD 412K was a 1972 Ford R192 with Duple Viceroy Express body. It was new to Wainfleet of Nuneaton. It is seen here outside the swimming pool at Buckie.

Irene's Coaches/Newmachar Coaches, Newmachar. The company subsequently changed the name to Newmachar Coaches. One of the more recent vehicles operated was E997 NMK, acquired from Moffat & Williamson in 2000. This Plaxton-bodied Leyland Tiger was new in 1988 to Armchair of Brentford.

J & L Coaches, Fraserburgh. I imagine this would have been a painful journey for the driver and his passengers, all the way from Rosehearty to Glasgow on 21 May 1983 in this 1965 Plaxton-bodied Bedford SB5.

J & L Coaches, Fraserburgh. Turbo Power and International Crusader – pretty optimistic for a nine-year-old Ford R1114. This Plaxton-bodied coach was new to Parks of Hamilton.

J & L Coaches, Fraserburgh. The Midnight Flyer and International Voyager! A most impressive description for a six-year-old Bedford YMT. OCN 906R was new in 1977 to Moordale of Newcastle and is seen in Glasgow on 21 May 1983.

JW Coaches, Banchory. JW Coaches was established in 1992, following the takeover of the Clark's of Banchory business. One of the vehicles inherited was 5696 KZ, a 1973 Plaxton-bodied Leyland Leopard, new to Bonas of Coventry as GWK 173L.

Jim's Coaches, Fochabers. Acquired in 2000 from Prentice of Haddington, this 1985 Van Hool T815 is seen on the premises of Elgin-based commercial-vehicle repairers, Baillie Brothers. It was new as C86 HCX to the Traject Group.

John C. Keir, Glass. Keir's was another company to start off as car and taxi hirers. Coaches were acquired as more people wanted to travel, and an early purchase was Duple-bodied Bedford OB CBV 857. After being withdrawn for service, it languished at the Glass depot before being sold for preservation. It has since been broken for spares.

John C. Keir, Glass. The newest addition to the fleet is YN61 EOM, a 2012 Plaxton-bodied Volvo B7R, new to Anderson of Bermondsey.

Keir's Coaches, Kemnay. Originally based in Kemnay, the company moved to a new base on the outskirts of Kintore around 2002 to accommodate the increased coach fleet. One of the more unusual coaches to grace the fleet was F224 RJX, a 1989 DAF SBR3000, new to Cosgrove of Preston. Another rare vehicle in the photo is F867 TBP, apparently one of a small number of Robin Hood Krypton bodied Iveco mini coaches.

Keir's Coaches, Kemnay. One of the last acquisitions before the company changed hands was YN55 PZB, a 2005 Irizar-bodied Scania new to Weavaway of Newbury. The company was sold in 2010 and now trades as Premier Coaches.

Kineil Coaches, Fraserburgh/Elgin. Originally a motor trader, the company expanded into coaches in the late eighties. Early acquisitions were mainly second-hand Bedfords and Fords, including this 1974 Plaxton-bodied Ford R1114, bought from Alex Norrie of New Deer in 1992.

Kineil Coaches, Fraserburgh. As the company expanded, there was more emphasis on providing high-quality coaches, with Volvo Van Hool coaches being the preferred choice. A new depot was opened in Elgin following a successful school transport contract award. This also gave a base for the ever-increasing requirement for coaches to serve incoming cruise liners at Invergordon. Seen at the cruise liner terminal is PSU 755, a 1996 Van Hool Volvo B10M, previously N525 PYS, and new to Parks of Hamilton as HSK 647.

Kineil Coaches, Fraserburgh. Three new coaches have recently been added to the fleet, all carrying this new livery introduced for 2016. SF65 CZP, seen at the Elgin depot, is a VDL Bova.

Kirkpatrick's Coaches, Banchory. UMJ 349K was a 1972 Plaxton-bodied Ford R226, and is seen in Glasgow on 10 May 1986 with football supporters attending the Scottish Cup final.

Kirkpatrick's Coaches, Banchory. A later addition to the fleet was WSC 32R, a 1977 Bedford VAS5 new to Silver Fox of Edinburgh.

John Lawrence, Cullen. I guess this would have been the first non-Alexander's bus I ever travelled on! Spending the first thirteen years of my life in Cullen, this Commer Commando would have taken me on Sunday School picnics.

Law's Coaches, Aberdeen. Nothing changes – even in 1983, drivers arriving at high-profile events such as cup finals would be greeted by enforcement officers. The officer appears to be checking the fuel of TFV 69J, perhaps to ensure no red diesel was being used. This 1971 Bedford SB5 was new to Enterprise of Blackpool.

Law's Coaches, Aberdeen. The driver of AEC Reliance FJP 501 appears to be getting an escort from police top-brass on arrival in Glasgow on 19 May 1984. New to Smith's of Wigan in 1960, it was re-bodied with this Plaxton body in 1973.

E & M Lees, Lumphanan. ELZ 1566, originally E684 NNH, was a 1988 Leyland Tiger with Jonckheere body. It is seen departing Aboyne Academy in June 2005.

E & M Lees, Lumphanan. Seen on the promenade at Aberdeen in 2009 is former Hutchison of Overtown Van Hool-bodied Volvo B10M, registered P502 VUS when new in 1997.

R. W. Love, Elgin. Robert 'Bobby' Love started his Elgin-based coach business in 1981. Bought for a school contract to Forres Academy, WSC 34R was a Plaxton-bodied Bedford YMT, new in 1977 to Silver Fox in Edinburgh. Noteworthy is the aluminium panel in place of a side window.

R. W. Love, Elgin. This tidy 1976 Duple-bodied Bedford YLQ was acquired primarily for hire work rather than for schools. It was new to Jolly Bus of South Hylton.

Low's Coaches, Tomintoul. This former Alexander's 1934 Leyland LT5B P159 was acquired by Low's in 1948.

Low's Coaches, Tomintoul. The company held the road service licence for the Tomintoul–Keith service. In this late seventies' view, their 1964 Duple-bodied Bedford SB5 sits in Keith Square prior to taking up the homeward journey.

Low's Coaches, Tomintoul. The company would change hands in the eighties, with the new owner adding to the fleet and trading as Glenlivet and District, as well as Low's Coaches. One of the vehicles added to the fleet was FHS 740X, an ex-Parks of Hamilton Duple bodied Volvo B10M. The company ceased trading during 1990.

MacLean's Coaches, Portknockie. Another entrant to the local coach scene in the early nineties was Portknockie-based MacLeans Coaches. One of their earliest acquisitions was ENJ 923V, acquired from Rennies of Dunfermline. This 1979 Plaxton-bodied Leyland Leopard had been new to Southdown, and had at some point been fitted with a more modern lower front panel.

MacLean's Coaches, Portknockie. A more impressive acquisition in 1992 was XRC 487, a 1985 Van Hool-bodied Volvo B10M. It is seen here on a private hire at Ayr racecourse. It was acquired from Pride of the Clyde.

Mair's Coaches, Aberdeen. Mair's Coaches was another company to expand on the back of the oil boom in Aberdeen during the seventies, making them an attractive proposition when Grampian were looking to expand in the eighties. This 1978 Plaxton-bodied Ford R1114 had departed the fleet before the takeover.

Mair's Coaches, Aberdeen. New coaches as well as second-hand acquisitions were purchased to meet client demands. One such vehicle was LSS 915W, a 1980 Caetano-bodied Volvo B58. This coach did survive into Grampian ownership days, repainted into a red-and-cream livery and reregistered PSU 629. It would see further service with a Cleveland operator, reregistered to PSO 85W. It is seen here in Glasgow in May 1985.

Maynes Coaches, Buckie. Maynes would be the longest-established independent operator in the area, starting coach hire in 1947 with one Bedford OB coach. To mark their fiftieth anniversary in 1997, they acquired a similar coach to the first one operated, KKN 752, a Duple-bodied Bedford OB. It regularly appears at special events in the local area.

Maynes Coaches, Buckie. The company have, over the years, bought many impressive vehicles, but the one that probably got most attention was 'Flipper', a 1998 Scania Irizar carrying a livery designed by local school pupils.

Maynes Coaches, Buckie. KM07 GSM would have been one of the last new deliveries to carry the familiar blue livery. This 2007 Volvo B12B with Van Hool body is seen on rail replacement work at Elgin station.

Maynes Coaches, Buckie. A new silver livery was adopted for the 2010 deliveries, as shown on this Neoplan coach, seen at the Southport coach park in July 2013.

Maynes Coaches, Buckie. Deliveries for 2016 include a further Neoplan carrying the branding for David Urquhart tours, and the company's first new Mercedes Tourismo, liveried for tour work in Orkney. A further two Tourismo coaches are due for delivery at the time of writing.

McIntyre's Coaches, Aberdeen. Based in Old Aberdeen, McIntyre's operated a mix of contract, private hire and tour work. OFR 928T was a 1979 Duple-bodied Volvo B58, new to Battersby Silver-Grey of Morecambe. It is seen in Glasgow with Aberdeen football supporters in May 1986.

McIntyre's Coaches, Aberdeen. Purchased new in 1980, this Caetano-bodied Volvo B58 is seen on the Shiprow tour stance before setting off on a local afternoon or evening tour.

Meldrum Motors, Oldmeldrum. Seen during the late seventies parked up at the back of the filling station in Oldmeldrum is COA 898C, a 1965 Duple-bodied Ford. It appears to be out of service at the time it was photographed.

Meldrum Motors, Oldmeldrum. This newer coach was, however, still in service at that time. DUP 848G was a 1969 Plaxton-bodied Bedford VAM70.

Milne's Coaches, New Byth. BMC was a name synonymous with the British vehicle industry, but the name disappeared as part of the restructuring of British Leyland. BMC Turkey reintroduced the BMC name when it started exporting vehicles to the UK in 2002. One such vehicle was this BMC Probus.

Milne's Coaches, New Byth. Parked at the New Byth depot on a dreich day was MIL 5714, a 1998 Van Hool-bodied Volvo B10M, new as R203 MGA to MacPhail of Newarthill.

W & R Murray, Alford. Another late seventies' view – MRS 519 was a 1959 Bedford SB3 with Duple body and appeared still to be operational when photographed. It is recorded as being new with Simpson of Aberdeen.

W & R Murray, Alford. Parked at the same spot but at a much later date is Duple Viceroy bodied Bedford VAM5 CTC 187E.

M. W. Nicoll, Laurencekirk. Seen at their impressive Laurencekirk depot are three Van Hool Volvo coaches, used primarily for school contract work and private hires. A20 MWN was originally H197 DVM in the Shearings fleet, E996 FRA was originally E310 OPR in the Excelsior fleet, while M275 TSB retains its original registration when new to Crawford of Neilston.

M. W. Nicoll, Laurencekirk. Two new Alexander Enviro 200 service saloons were purchased in 2011 to operate services in the Mearns area. YX11 CRV and YX11 CRZ are seen at the depot.

Nobles Motor Services, Fraserburgh. Seen outside Kenny Noble's Stevenson Road garage is RNP 955P, a 1976 Plaxton-bodied Volvo B58 acquired from Charlie Scott t/a Rosehearty Coaches.

Norrie's Coaches, New Deer. An early acquisition in the Norrie fleet was AWO 141B, a 1964 Bedford SB5 with Plaxton body, new to Parfitt of Rhymney Valley.

Norrie's Coaches, New Deer. FUJ 905V was a regular performer on the Buchan Link service between Fraserburgh and Aberdeen in the mid-to-late eighties. This Duple-bodied Bedford YMT was new to the Whittle group. It is seen at the Castlegate in Aberdeen.

Peace Coaches, Aberdeen. Initially set up in 1986 as a joint venture with J. D. Peace (Orkney), the company came under the sole ownership of the Collie's in 1994, but continues to trade as Peace Coaches. An early acquisition was this rare 12-metre Alexander-bodied AEC Reliance. It was new to the Road Transport Industry Training Board and was based at their Livingston training facility.

Peace Coaches, Aberdeen. In the early days vehicles would be transferred between the Aberdeen and Orkney operations. One transfer to Aberdeen was former MacBrayne Bedford SB5 PGD 216F. It was subsequently used as a flower pot showroom in Fochabers.

Peace Coaches, Aberdeen. The company was originally based at Bucksburn adjacent to the now-closed Clover Leaf Hotel, where these four coaches were photographed. KKV 698V was a 1980 Plaxton-bodied Volvo B58; LCX 159W was a 1981 Plaxton-bodied AEC Reliance, subsequently sold to Hardie's of Aberchirder, and EWW 214T a 1979 Plaxton-bodied Leyland Leopard, new to Wallace Arnold, and subsequently sold to Maynes of Buckie. At the end of the line-up is LVA 261L, a 1973 Ford R1014, acquired from Masons of Bo'ness at the same time as the AEC and Leopard. It subsequently went to Brian Gray for PCV driving training.

Peace Coaches, Aberdeen. As up to date as it gets, these two new VDL Bova coaches had just been delivered when photographed and had not entered service. They were photographed at the Echt depot, the home of the company since moving out of Aberdeen.

Peem's Coaches, Insch. Originally a taxi and minibus operator, Jim 'Peem' Sutherland expanded into coaches in the early nineties. One of his purchases was this tidy Plaxton-bodied Volvo B58, new as GDS 403T to Southern of Barrhead in 1979.

Peem's Coaches, Insch. UIB 1579 was quite a rare coach. It was a DAF MB2000, with Belgium-built LAG body. New to Grangeburn of Motherwell in 1985, it was originally registered C570 RPM.

Phillip Coaches, Alford. Philip Coaches was another company that started off with minibuses, expanding into full-size coaches around 2002. KBZ 5749 was a Duple-bodied Volvo B58, new in 1984 as A287 FEC to Brown of Ambleside.

Phillip Coaches, Alford. One of the last acquisitions before the company ceased trading in 2014 was WA09 HTV, a former D Coaches Bova Majiq acquired in 2011, following the collapse of the Welsh-based tour company.

Premier Coaches, Kintore. On acquiring the Keir's of Kemnay business in 2010, the new owner renamed the company to Premier Coaches, and adopted a new livery for the entire fleet. An early purchase was this former Philip of Alford Jonckheere bodied Volvo B10M, still carrying the all-white livery from its previous owner.

Premier Coaches, Kintore. The new owner has invested in modern executive-style coaches, including BF63 ZTE, a former Bennetts of Warrington 2013 Mercedes Caetano Levante, used by Bennetts on National Express contract services.

Reid's Coaches, Rhynie. Seen inside the garage at Rhynie in the late seventies is 640 HGB, a 1963 Plaxton-bodied Bedford SB5, new to McQuatter of Glasgow.

Reid's Coaches, Rhynie. Over the years, Reid's have operated a few double-deckers, including PBN 668, VRS 321 and GRS 119E. The last double-decker purchase was GOG 548N, a 1975 Daimler Fleetline, new to West Midland PTE. It is seen here at Rhynie, having been reregistered HSK 805. It would see further service with Watermill Coaches.

Reid's Coaches, Rhynie. This 2005 image shows one of the last full-size coaches to be purchased by Reid's before they reduced their operations to minibuses. HSK 816 was originally new to Whyte's of Newmachar as N83 LSE, a 1996 Caetano-bodied Volvo B10M. It is seen here operating a school contract from the Gordon Schools in Huntly.

Robb's of Brechin, Brechin. Although based out of the area covered by this book, Robb's operated into the Grampian area on school and subsidised service work. The fact that Mike Robb operated this former Alexander M Type coach makes his inclusion all the more worthy. HOI 2319 was originally registered HSD 706N when new to Western SMT in 1975 for the overnight service to London. The striking M Type body sits on a Volvo B58 chassis.

Roberts of Rothiemay, Rothiemay. George Roberts acquired the Robb of Rothiemay business in 1985. As well as the garage and filling station, Robb operated one coach, latterly a Ford R1014 registered PSN 93M. On expanding the business the Roberts were one of the first of the nineties era operators to utilise double-deckers for school contracts, acquiring two former Tayside Alexander bodied Volvo Ailsa deckers in the form of NSP 327R and 328R. The former is seen outside the garage at Rothiemay.

Roberts of Rothiemay, Rothiemay. For a contract requiring a low-floor vehicle, Roberts acquired this Optare Alero PN03 UGA, new to West Lancashire Dial-a-Ride.

Roberts of Rothiemay, Rothiemay. 2012 saw the company end bus and coach operations. VIL 4844 had departed the fleet before then. New as M104 CCD, it was a former Stagecoach 1995 Dennis Javelin. It is now in County Carlow, registered 95-CW-1863, in use as a school bus with Eamonn Spruhan & Sons.

Robertson's Coaches, Cuminestown. Seen in the garage at Cuminestown is W466 RKS, a Spanish-built Ferqui Solero-bodied Mercedes 112OL, new to Dublin-based Shamrocker Adventures as 00-D-45665.

Robertson's Coaches, Cuminestown. More mundane in the fleet was GIL 8044, a 1981 Plaxton Viewmaster-bodied Volvo B58, new as SLH 5W to Albatross of Brentford. It seen in Buckie on a private hire.

Roger's Coaches, Longside. A mid-seventies image of Robin Roger's MFD 500E, a 1967 Duple Viceroy-bodied Ford R192.

Roger's Coaches, Longside. The business was sold to Peter Cowe, who continued to trade as Rogers's Coaches. The company started a competing service on the Peterhead–Aberdeen corridor but, after fierce retaliation from Stagecoach, the service was eventually cancelled. The ACE – Aberdeen Commuter Express – name was adopted for the service. NIW 4582 carried the ACE branding during its time on the service. This Plaxton-bodied DAF was new as VSA 473X in 1982.

W. J. Ross, Dinnet. As well as operating the filling station at Dinnet, Bill Ross also operated coaches. BAR 825F is seen in Glasgow in May 1984. This Plaxton-bodied AEC Reliance was new in 1968.

W. J. Ross, Dinnet. Deeside was a favoured destination for tour companies such as Wallace Arnold and Shearings. They would hire in Bill Ross to provide a tour on the day their own driver rested. This view catches one of Ross's coaches on such a hire, coming into Banchory and no doubt letting the passengers enjoy an afternoon tea or whatever in the town centre. NRO 252V was a 1980 Duple-bodied Bedford YMT.

R. S. Coaches, Sauchen. Initially operating minibuses, RS expanded into coaches around 2000 and have over the years operated some exotic motors such as Neoplan and Van Hool T818 double-decker coaches. The fleet today is more standard, however, and includes N736 FJC, a Plaxton-bodied Volvo B10M recently acquired from Stuarts of Carluke. It was new to KMP of Llanberis as N77 KMP.

R. S. Coaches, Sauchen. JIL 2949 is a Plaxton-bodied Scania K93, new in 1990 to Shearings Coaches. It has had a non-standard front lower panel fitted at some point.

R. S. Coaches, Sauchen. This former Dublin Bus Volvo Olympian was acquired for a school contract in Aberdeenshire, but has since left the fleet and now operates with Diamond Coaches of Rushden.

Shearer's Coaches, Huntly. E793 MSE was new to Glennie's of Keith in 1987. This Duple-bodied Bedford YNT then passed to Shearer's in 1991. It was sold to Tomish Training in Inverness for PCV driver training in 2006 and subsequently reregistered to LIL 5997.

Shearer's Coaches, Huntly. In 2005 Shearer's were operating two former MOD Wadham Stringer bodied Dennis Javelin coaches. YIL 2252 was formerly ER 83 AA during its MOD days, but was registered N738 PAE when sold by the MOD.

Shirran Coaches, Lumsden. A former member of the fleet OSL 3N was a 1974 Duple-bodied Ford R1114, new to Mackie of Alloa. I recall seeing it again when owned by Victoria Coaches in Peterhead, by which time it had been fitted with the engine from a Volvo F86 truck.

Shirran Coaches, Lumsden. Probably the last Ford coach to operate in this area was FFH 721T, a 1979 Duple-bodied Ford R1114.

Shirran Coaches, Lumsden. Carrying a traditional Aberdeenshire registration is current fleet member VAV 552, originally N936 RBC. It is a 1996 Jonckheere-bodied Volvo B10M, new to Clyde Coast of Ardrossan.

Simpson's Coaches, Rosehearty. There has been a number of generations of Simpsons associated with this company. One of the earlier ones operated this Tilling Stevens, seen here having run off the road. Apparently it had been 'borrowed' by youths who did not want to walk home after a local dance.

Simpson's Coaches, Rosehearty. During the sixties and seventies, the company was heavily involved with the transportation of fishermen from north-east ports to the west coast of Scotland and, at times, as far south as the Devon and Cornwall ports. Typical of the vehicles acquired at that time was SRS 389R, a 1977 Plaxton-bodied Bedford YLQ.

Simpson's Coaches, Rosehearty. Today the company is owned by Ronald Simpson, who currently favours the Neoplan Tourliner. Here, five of the fleet are lined up ready for an early morning departure.

R. A. Simpson, Huntly. Although based in Huntly, the company also had a garage next to the Forgue Emporium. This Plaxton-bodied Bedford YRQ was purchased new in 1975.

R. A. Simpson, Huntly. BCP 125V was a Plaxton-bodied Bedford YMT, new in 1980 to a Sheffield-based operator. After withdrawal by Simpson, it passed to MacDonald of South Uist in 1988.

Smith's Coaches (Central Coaches), Keith. Vehicles from this fleet have displayed both Smith's Coaches' and Central Coaches' names over the years. This one, however, is seen after being sold on as a mobile shop but, as it was quite unique, I felt it appropriate to include. FSE 1F was a Martin Walker bodied Austin J2.

Smith's Coaches (Central Coaches), Keith. New in 1981, PSE 468W was a Plaxton-bodied Ford. R1114.

Smith's Coaches (Central Coaches), Keith. Seen at the Keith depot when newly acquired in 1993 is former Kings Ferry Caetano-bodied DAF MB230 G999 OKK. It now resides on a farm on the outskirts of Keith, in use as a store shed.

Smith's Coaches (Central Coaches), Keith. Seen departing Elgin bus station July 2011 on the service to Tomintoul is rare Berkhof-bodied short wheelbase Volvo B10M, badged as a B9.

R. E. Stables, Newmill, Keith. January 2010 saw some of the worst snowfall the north-east has encountered for a number of years. This image of Stables NUI2 420 hopefully conveys how bad it was. I think the mid-morning temperature was -16 °C!

R. E. Stables, Newmill, Keith. A recent addition to the fleet is former McCarthy of Macclesfield Plaxton-bodied Volvo B12M.

R. E. Stables, Newmill, Keith. During March and April the area can still get a covering of snow, as seen in this March 2016 image. Two of the current fleet sit outside the depot. Both are Jonckheere-bodied Volvo coaches, and both carry personalised RES plates.

Star Coaches, Aberdeen. Star Coaches, part of an Aberdeen-based taxi group, acquired this former Bluebird Buses Dodge S56 minibus for private hire work. It was new to Central Scottish in 1986.

James Stewart, Portlethen. Two of the final fleet at Hill of Findon, just before the owners retired in 2005. E433 YSU was a 1988 Mercedes 609D, with twenty-seven-seat Scott body, while N245 WDO was a 1995 Mercedes 410D with sixteen-seat Autobus body.

James Stewart, Portlethen. The owners, Jim and Mabel, pose together on 2 June 2005, just before their final few weeks on their longstanding school runs.

Strathdee's Coaches, Inverurie. Strathdee was a one-bus operation, started in 1975 when MGD 854P, a Duple-bodied Bedford VAS5, was bought new. A larger second-hand coach was acquired in the form of LUX 537P. This was a 1976 Duple-bodied Bedford YRQ.

Tait's Coaches, Newmachar. As far as I can recall, Fred Tait only operated two vehicles, a rare Wrights-bodied Bedford YMP and this 1988 Toyota, which was new to Long of Salsburgh and saw further service after Tait's with Peace Coaches in Orkney.

Victoria Coaches, Peterhead. PRG 40J was a 1970 Alexander-bodied AEC Reliance, new to Aberdeen Corporation. Victoria acquired it in 1990 from Grampian Fire Brigade, who had used it for staff transport between training centres. It is now preserved in its original Aberdeen colours.

Victoria Coaches, Peterhead. Robbie Smith sold the business in 1998, but the new owner retained the Victoria name and adopted a new livery, as shown on CXI 4526. This was a Plaxton-bodied Volvo B58, new to West Yorkshire PTE as LUB 507P.

Victoria Coaches, (Smith/Mowat) Peterhead. Added to the fleet in 2007 was Van Hool-bodied Volvo B10M NIW 252. It was new in 1999 as 2RWM in the Parks of Hamilton fleet.

Victoria Coaches, (Duncan) Macduff. 21 May 1983 and another load of Aberdeen Football Club supporters arrive in Glasgow. RCN 374S was a 1977 Plaxton-bodied Bedford YMT, new to Tyne and Wear PTE, but acquired from J & L Coaches, Rosehearty, in 1984.

Victoria Coaches, (Duncan) Macduff. E763 HJF is seen at the Banff Academy bus parking area. It was a 1988 Duple-bodied Bedford YNV, new to Reynolds of Maerdy.

W & G Coaches, Cuminestown. W & G Coaches acquired this Caetano-bodied DAF MB200 from Cruickshank's of Ellon in 1998. It was new in 1985 as B669 GBD with Trathens.

Watermill Coaches, Fraserburgh. The company was founded in 1979 by the present owners and have built up a significant operation with depots in Fraserburgh, Peterhead and Ellon. This one-time Brown of Macduff Volvo B58 is seen in Glasgow on 28 February 1987.

Watermill Coaches, Fraserburgh. The company has operated quite a few deckers over the years, including examples of Daimler Fleetline, Leyland Atlantean and Volvo Ailsa. Probably the only MCW Metrobus to operate in the area was JIL 8207. It was new to South Yorkshire PTE in 1983 as A113 XWE.

Watermill Coaches, Fraserburgh. Seen when new at the Ythanbank quarry depot is YP52 KRG, a 2002 seventy-seat Plaxton-bodied Volvo B7R.

Whyte's Coaches, Newmachar. Over the years Whyte's have been primarily a private hire and tour company, supplemented with a small amount of school contract work. They have also been involved in operating express services on hire to the likes of Stagecoach. This particular coach was operating a supermarket contract when photographed. It is a Caetano-bodied Volvo B10m, new to Parks of Hamilton in 1986.

Whyte's Coaches, Newmachar. Seen promoting their 2007 tour programme at the Maynes of Buckie sixtieth-anniversary open day is SV06 CEJ, a 2006 Bova FHD12.